MAGIC ISLANDS

Jamie Owen

MAGIC ISLANDS

GOMER

First Impression 2002
Second Impression 2003

ISBN 1 84323 190 5

© text: Jamie Owen
© photographs: Aspect Television,
           unless otherwise noted
© watercolour sketches: John Rogers

Printed in Wales at
Gomer Press, Llandysul, Ceredigion

for my family and friends

CONTENTS

ACKNOWLEDGEMENTS

I should like to express my sincere thanks to: the crew
of *Mascotte* – Tony and Will Winter, Mags and John
Hart; the islanders and boatmen of Anglesey, Bardsey,
Skomer, Ramsey, Caldey and Lundy; the people of
Penarth, Tenby, Neyland, Fishguard, Holyhead and
Port Dinorwic for their hospitality; everyone at Aspect
Television – Rob Finighan, Sara Allen, Chris Howells,
Mary Adams and Jon Rees; Martyn Ingram, Clare
Hudson, Mark o'Callaghan, Gail Morris Jones, Julie
Barton, Tony O'shaughnessy and Dewi Vaughan Owen
at the BBC; Pete Telfer, Martin Cavaney, Nona Rees,
Mike Edmonds and Phil Harries for photographs;
Christine Evans and Raymond Garlick for permission to
include their poems; Sir Kyffin Williams for permission
to reproduce a painting; John Rogers for his painting of
the Garland Stone, Skomer Island, and for the
watercolour details from his sketchbooks which appear
from chapter to chapter; Phil Carradice for all his help
in the preparation of this book; Elgan Davies of the
Welsh Books Council for the design; Mairwen Prys
Jones and the staff of Gomer Press.

P R E F A C E

WHEN I WAS A LITTLE BOY, Mr Cole spent many fruitless afternoons teaching us how to paint the view of Milford Haven that we could see through the classroom window. Sadly, my tankers, coasters and yachts would never have been very seaworthy. My end of term report always said, 'Could do better' or 'Too much time day dreaming'. I was never any good at art – and it was true, I did spend far too much time imagining the places to where the ships were sailing rather than noticing their lines and silhouettes.

Years later, when I first set eyes on *Mascotte*, the 60-foot Bristol Channel pilot cutter where I would soon be spending many hours, I remembered where I'd last seen a boat like this. She looked exactly like the sailing boat a child would draw – one mast, lots of rigging, three sails and acres of polished wood, heavily decorated with brass.

This 1904 sailing boat was to be home for the summer – a voyage, sailing around the coast and islands of Wales. It was a journey *Mascotte* would have made countless times when she was in her prime.

It wasn't an epic dash across oceans or wild seas, more a journey home, to the people and places which, though right on my doorstep, were strangely unfamiliar. Why 'Magic Islands'? Simple. From Lundy to Anglesey, from Caldey and Skomer up to Bardsey, in storms and brilliant sunshine, through hail, wind and rain, I was transfixed by their beauty and beguiled by the people who live there. They are 'Magic Islands'.

1 SETTING OUT

WALKING ACROSS *MASCOTTE'S DECK* is like stepping back in time. A hundred years ago harbour pilots used boats like this one to meet large vessels out at sea, vessels that were heading for the thriving ports of south Wales, shipping coal and steel across the world. The pilots were self-employed and highly competitive men, racing each other to the approaching ships to win prized contracts from their captains. Whoever piloted a vessel into port also won the right to take her back out to sea, so it was important to get there first. We do not intend to bring the same urgency to *Mascotte's* voyage this time, I'm pleased to say.

I go backwards down the ladder, into the darkness of the ship's panelled saloon. Tom Cox has come to wish me well. Tom's great grandfather built the *Mascotte* a hundred years ago.

Her life as a pilot cutter did not last long but it was certainly action-packed. She worked out of Newport and Barry between 1904 and 1914: indeed, the huge letter N, for the port of Newport, is still emblazoned on her mainsail. In those days she would have been crewed by one man and a boy – as well as the pilot, of course. It must have been a hard life. Looking at Tom, however, it doesen't seem to have done him much harm. Sea water must run in the veins.

'Fourth generation of harbour pilots,' he tells me. 'My father, grandfather, great grandfather all plied their trade in these waters – in all kinds of weather.'

Boarding at Penarth

Mascotte's sail boasts
an N for Newport

He chuckles at that and winks his way through stories of *Mascotte* pounded by raging seas and haunted by dozens of sea ghosts.

'Ghosts?' I ask, tentatively. 'Whose ghosts?'

Tom smiles wickedly and inclines his head towards some vague, ill-defined spot at the foot of the companionway.

'My grandfather's ghost. He was a bit crazy, didn't tolerate fools gladly. Had to be – how can you say it? – the fastest pilot on the block. Three times he won the pilot cutter cup. But the family didn't like him much. Still, he was happy here, on the *Mascotte*. I think that's why it feels like he's still here.'

Tom goes on to tell us about some of the gales he encountered during his days at sea. It doesn't sound very reassuring. We listen and laugh and gaze apprehensively at the storm clouds out over the Bristol Channel.

Our first port of call is to be Lundy, some sixty miles away from Penarth, a journey that *Mascotte* has sailed a thousand times. The old pilots would sometimes loiter as far afield as Liverpool or Dover, waiting for a profitable cargo ship to guide into port. *Mascotte* would

On deck
and
eager to
be off

have spent many nights anchored beneath Lundy's cliffs, waiting for the storms to pass.

Yesterday's sailors had no VHF radio or satellite forecasting systems, just a weather eye and a barometer. We edge out of Penarth and make our way through the lock into a brown and angry Bristol Channel. Tom Cox doesn't need a shipping forecast: he's seen skies like this before – but he doesn't let on.

There are no electric winches to raise and lower the sails on *Mascotte*, so the first day's sail is arduous work. I don't think I have ever ached so much. The men who made their living on the pilot boats must have been robust characters. No doubt they would have laughed at my office hands, blistered and rope-burnt.

Our mainsail, foresail and jib are all raised, and freezing waves now smack into the bows of *Mascotte*. Oilskins keep the worst of the wind and waves at bay. My respect for the pilots increases with every hour that I grip the deck. Flatholm Island looms grey and menacing on the horizon, like a cold wet whale. Sadly, it is not Lundy – our destination still lies ten hours away. The first day's sailing soon turns into a test of endurance and I guess that none of us is relishing the cold hours ahead, even though none of us cares to admit it. The wind is westerly six, touching seven. That means 30 knots of wind on the anometer – and we are going head to wind in an ebb tide.

After only a few hours the meteorological office forecast of gale force 8 turns us back to Penarth. Though defeated, I am relieved – to put it mildly. We listen to the shipping forecast and hope that the gales will cease by the following day so that we can make the quick dash to Lundy. The apprehension is still there, even though we are anchored in Penarth's safe and protecting marina. I reckon that if I tried hard I would probably hear *Mascotte's* ghost laughing at my fear.

Below deck in the saloon, navigation charts and tide timetables give way to supper. There is ham, cheese, bread and wine – and more of Tom's terrible tales from the sea.

I climb into my cupboard bunk, its door halfway up the companionway wall. Freezing cold, still damp and exhausted from a hard day's sailing, I try to get comfortable. There's just enough room to lie flat. For what seems like hours I lie there, twisting and turning, the images of sea demons and phantom vessels crowding into my active but exhausted brain. As I finally drop off to sleep, water begins to drip over my back – a leak from the deck above. Aboard *Mascotte*, clearly, there is no escape from the sea, not even in your dreams.

Flatholm Island lies off the coast of Wales near Cardiff. According to legend two of the murderers of Archbishop Thomas Becket are buried there.

In the eighteenth century Flatholm was renowned as a haunt of smugglers and pirates. The most famous of these was Pasco Robinson who, for many years, terrorised the area in his 40-ton sloop adorned with the figurehead of a red mermaid.

2 A CHANGE OF PLAN

AFTER TWO DAYS holed up in Penarth, with the winds in the wrong direction for Lundy, we decide on a change of plan. There is a bit of a window in the weather so it's 'head west, young man', to Pembrokeshire. There's no sunshine but the wind allows us to sail at high tide, overnight, for Tenby. It's a twelve-hour sail and at ten we slip

Penarth
Marina

left
John Hart, old
sea-dog

right
Tony Winter,
Mascotte's
owner

ropes and head out into the Bristol Channel. The lights of Cardiff Bay mark out our passage. On a fair night this must be one of the most lovely journeys in Wales – tonight, with spray from the waves drenching us and with unseasonally cold temperatures, it has to be one of the loneliest.

We clip our safety harnesses to the deck to save falling into the swell. You wouldn't last long in there on a night like this. Just like it would have been back in 1904, when *Mascotte* made her maiden voyage, there are no lights on deck. Only those safety straps give us the confidence to stand upright – and even that is much against better judgement.

Trying to sleep in the bunk while the ship lurches onwards requires great concentration or considerable experience. I count the hours, rolling with the sea. They say darkness accelerates the perception of speed and we seem to be tearing towards Pembrokeshire on a beam reach. Tony Winter, *Mascotte*'s owner, and John Hart, the pilot, are the overnight watch.

'Get your heads down,' Tony tells us. 'We'll need you fit and well rested for tomorrow morning.'

We take his advice and try to sleep through our passage around the coast of south Wales.

The fort on St Catherine's Island at Tenby was originally intended as part of the defensive network for nearby Pembroke Dockyard. It was designed to house 11 guns and was manned by 60 artillerymen. The fort is just one of many Palmerston Follies along the coast of Wales – so called because by the time the money for their construction had been voted through Parliament and building begun, the danger they were meant to counter had long disappeared.

Three islands:
St Catherine's,
Caldey and
St Margaret's

Tenby
harbour

Mascotte as far marker for the Yacht Club

Caldey Island is a mile and a half in length, two thirds of a mile wide. It is made from Carboniferous Limestone and Old Red Sandstone. Unlike the other Welsh islands, much of the landmass slopes towards the mainland. This gives the land some protection and, as a consequence, Caldey is much more fertile than other islands.

Nash Point, Porthcawl, Port Talbot's raging chimneys, which fire the night sky, the blackness of Mumbles, Worm's Head, West Helwick buoy and Carmarthen Bay – all pass by to starboard while we lie in our bunks.

A needle shaft of light wakes me at a quarter to five. On deck it's a new, bright morning. I don't think there's any feeling in the world quite like sailing in silence, with no noise apart from the waves against the hull, watching in awe as tide and wind work their magic.

After twelve hours Tenby looms up before us. Our first islands, Caldey and St. Catherine's, are suddenly in our midst. At the invitation of the Coxswain, *Mascotte* inches towards the RNLI buoy, the only mooring big enough to take her weight. We dodge the lobster pots hurtling around in the waves and pick up the mooring.

Barefoot and bound for the Yacht Club

Sun breaks out across the harbour. After the rain, wind and freezing cold of the last two days it's a real joy to sit on the wooden deck and bathe in the morning heat. Tourists in their hired rowing boats, even fishermen and day-boats, pass close by for a closer look at us. Tenby Sailing Club request us to be their far marker for that evening's race and Tony Winter happily agrees. Meanwhile, it's time for some shore leave!

We leave *Mascotte* by tiny tender, with a precarious hundred yards to go to the beach.

Tony's words offer little comfort. 'Most of the losses connected on these pilot boats happened because of accidents in their tenders,' he tells us. 'Not on the boats themselves.'

I'm beginning to see why. Four of us hold grimly to the sides of a craft no bigger than a table-cloth and head shakily off towards the shore.

Lifeboat station at Tenby

Elegant Georgian architecture at Tenby

In the 1920s and '30s Tenby used to be the most westerly port of call for the famous White Funnel paddle steamers. The town's Royal Victoria Pier was demolished following the Second World War, however, and after that the paddlers had to use the tidal harbour. By the end of the 1950s they had ceased to call.

Tenby's gently shelving sands mean that it's too shallow to reach dry land so we take off our shoes and socks to wade the last few yards to shore. Smoke fills the air – the wonderful smell of roasting meat wafting around the ancient harbour walls. The warmest of welcomes awaits us in the Sailing Club, nestled into an ancient warehouse near the slipway. The view from the balcony is simply breathtaking: picture postcard stuff. Just along from the club, hiding in the harbour's arches, Pete's Plaice offers the day's catch. Lobster and mackerel prices are neatly chalked up on the door.

Alan Thomas is Tenby's lifeboat coxswain and skipper of the trip boat to Caldey. He's full of lovely stories about shipping sheep and cattle out to the island – with varying degrees of success.

'We were welding on a boat once,' he smiles, 'repair job, nothing too serious, out there on the island. One of the cows got a bit too interested in what we were doing. Took away all the usual, more accepted ways of roasting beef!'

Alan says that these days the lifeboat men have changed. Not their courage or dedication, just their jobs. Once the crews were all fishermen and professional boatmen. Now volunteers are as likely to be doctors, dentists and lawyers. Wherever they come from, though, and whatever their livelihood, their commitment is humbling.

The Sailing Club is packed full of kids who've been racing their dingies. I'd expected a stuffy and crusty old set, propping up the bar, wearing blazers and drinking pink gins. But the atmosphere here is young and thriving.

Eventually it's time to return to *Mascotte*. The tender is at the steps cut into the stone jetty. The harbour is now filling with the incoming tide. We edge our way through thousands of reflected lights on the surface of the water as St. Mary's spire stands proudly above the roofs of the town. The bells chime eleven as we turn in for the night, ready for Caldey Island in the morning.

3 CALDEY

WE SLIP OUR MOORINGS in early sunshine, the sky a thousand shades of white. At this moment I don't think I would wish to be anywhere else. Tenby's ancient harbour is already bustling with fishermen and sleepy-eyed skippers – just as it has been for centuries.

It's only a short hop from Tenby harbour over to Caldey Island. *Mascotte* draws ten feet beneath the waves so there is no chance of reaching the island's jetty – and that's reserved for the island boat, anyway. Back to the tender again! Isn't it strange how distance, any distance, looks much shorter when you don't have to row?

Rowing to Caldey

Caldey's sandy beach and short slipway already have a gaggle of passengers this morning, all waiting for the Tenby boat. There are clergymen returning refreshed from 'retreat', families heading home to the mainland, islanders going shopping for the day.

Tying up the tender on the beach, I remember the countless times we made this trip as kids, my mother in her wide, floppy sunhat. We lost

Caldey was once known as the Isle of Saints, a tribute to the religious men who made the place their home. Traces of earlier habitation have been found, and there was a settlement on the island dating to 300 – 400 AD. Bones of animals like woolly rhinoceros, giant ox and cave bear, as well as pieces of clay pots have been found in caves on the island, along with the remains of ancient fires.

my brother Richard here once. A monk gave him a bar of chocolate to stop him crying and put him on the flat roof of the shop so that we'd see him as we searched. I remember my father stepping awkwardly off the boat, lumbering heavily up the slip – already too long in the sun. I wish I'd known then how much I'd miss him now.

Caldey is a curious mix of paradise and junkyard. A myriad of scrap vehicles litter your arrival. There's even a DUKW from the Second World War. Cars, whose legal mainland tenures have long expired, find an after-life here – motor heaven, without tax or MOT.

England are playing in the World Cup this weekend. As I walk past the monastery a cry suddenly goes up from inside the building. England has scored. Whoever said that religious life is without earthly reward? This is also the weekend of the Queen's Golden Jubilee and the islanders are planning a tea party later in the afternoon.

Veronica Cattini

Rita Cunningham with her peacocks.

Veronica and John Cattini's house is set in beautiful gardens, sheltered from Irish Sea storms by tall trees. Veronica is baking for the party – cheese straws, Welsh cakes and flapjacks. A kettle on the Aga provides endless cups of tea while she tells me about her thirty years on the island. It seems to have been an idyllic life, enjoyed by her children

Village life:
Rita
Cunningham
on her
tractor

and the handful of other kids who have grown up here. Now that the children have gone, I ask, would they leave Caldey, rather than grow old there?

'No chance,' she says, shaking her head. 'John and I are staying here, whatever comes, whatever happens. This is home.'

Rita Cunningham must be in her eighties. In an ancient farmhouse on the far side of the island she is feeding her hens and peacocks. What does she remember of the Queen's Coronation fifty years ago, I ask? She smiles. She has no recollection of the 1950s. In those days she was a nun in a closed convent community. Now, she lives here, playing the organ in the monastery, managing the island's water supply and driving her small tractor across the rugged terrain, terrifying visitors.

The Jubilee Tea Party is quite unlike anything I've ever experienced before. All the islanders, including the monks, gather together in a former chicken shed that is now the village hall to celebrate the last fifty years. There is no electric amplifier or taped music but everyone has brought a dish of food. The trestle table groans under the weight of cheese and pineapple, sausages on sticks, sandwiches, cakes and tea.

In a society where, these days, no-one sings unaccompanied in

The famous John Paul Jones, founder of the American navy, has connections with Caldey. Jones Bay on the island is supposed to be the spot where he came ashore for water while cruising in the Bristol Channel during the American War of Independence.

Legend declares that Abbot Pŷr, after whom Caldey takes its Welsh name (Ynys Bŷr), was drowned when he fell into a pond in a drunken stupor.

public, there is a certain awkwardness at first – at least amongst us visitors. We all stare, unconvinced, at the song sheets we've been given. Soon, we lose our embarrassment and join in a fragile unison. One of the monks sings a beautiful solo. What a strange place this is but then, at the same time, I can't help wondering who has worked out the better life, me or them?

On the village green, the Golden Jubilee Memorial is unveiled. I ask one of the younger monks, Brother Francis – who must be about the same age as me – whether or not he is lonely in a monastery of old men.

'I've got the love of God,' he smiles, serenely. 'I couldn't want for anything else.'

His conviction unnerves me, somewhat. Such absolute certainty.

On the beach that evening I come across a slick of tiny dead jelly fish. The slick is a yard wide, creatures blown off course and washed up on a beach, a world away from home.

The beach at evening

4 MORNING WATCH

THE NEXT MORNING I stand in the brittle early morning sunshine on the wooden deck of *Mascotte* and try to think about the island that lies before me. Nobody else is awake yet. The boat seems as empty as the *Marie Celeste* and there is such a perfect stillness that I can almost understand what it was that brought the holy men to this island in the first place.

Caldey is only two miles from Tenby but it could be a world away. It's a small island, covering about 650 acres and rising to a maximum height of just 180 feet. In the summer the climate is almost Mediterranean but in winter fierce gales and storms sweep in across its low, flat land.

When I was a child, at school in nearby Pembroke Dock, we were taught about the monks of Caldey. Everyone knew about them, regarded them almost as a trophy.

'We have monks in Pembrokeshire!' we used to tell people less fortunate than ourselves, visitors and relatives who appeared, perhaps, once or twice a year. 'Bet you don't have monks where you live.'

Not many people actually went to see them, however. And now, with hindsight, that seems something of a shame.

The monastery is the most significant building on the island. It's

Moored, early
morning, off
Caldey

The monastery

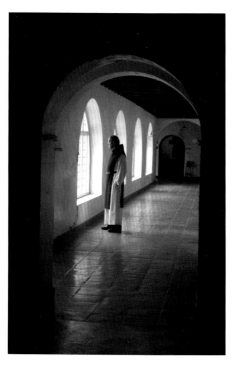

A simple setting for contemplation

Whilst the Welsh name for Caldey is Ynys Bŷr, its English name derives from the Norse word 'keld' meaning 'spring' – clearly the raiding Norsemen of the 'Dark Ages' were used to coming ashore on the island to find fresh water.

Communication between Caldey and the mainland has never been easy. There have been several well-loved boats operating between the island and Tenby, the most famous being the *Firefly* which was wrecked in 1916. A telephone cable was laid on the sea bed but this snapped in the years prior to the Second World War. It was not repaired until the early 1960s.

relatively modern but Caldey has had a long connection with organised religion. In Welsh, the island is known as Ynys Bŷr. That name commemorates the Celtic missionary or holy man St Pŷr. He came here in the 6th century, founding a community of monks who seemed destined to suffer at the hands of warlike Vikings and Norsemen. Despite being raided, massacred and generally beaten about, the monks remained, obviously fortified and strengthed by their faith.

In 1136 the island was given to the Benedictines of St. Dogmaels. They built the first priory and also St. Illtud's church, remaining in possession of Caldey until Henry VIII dissolved the monasteries in 1536. The other church on the island is known as St. David's and, like St. Illtud's, this fell into disrepair after Henry's edict. The two churches were restored in 1900.

Standing on *Mascotte's* deck this morning it's the present monastery and its superb Romanesque architecture that impresses. I've seen it before, of course, many times. Built between 1910 and 1913 by Anglican Benedictines, it must have cost them a fortune – particularly as they then went on to buy the island itself. The monks soon got themselves into serious financial difficulties but whether or not this was due to the cost of creating the wonderful monastery I can't say.

Whatever the reason, the Benedictines moved to Prinknash in Gloucester and sold the island to the Cistercian Order. It was in 1929 that a small contingent of Cistercians Trappists – a silent Order – arrived from Belgium. Their descendents are still in possession of the monastery today.

And yet Caldey is more than just a monastery. The island has always been farmed. In the long interregnum between the dissolution of the monasteries in 1536 and the return of the monks at the beginning of the 20th century the islanders had no alternative but to try and force a living from the soil. The monks themselves have always supported their lifestyle by farming of one sort or another. Yet it has not been easy and

Farming on Caldey

these days the islanders tend to rely on the tourist trade; in the case of the monks, the production of perfume from the gorse and lavender on the island helps them make a living. Communication with the mainland has always been a problem – although on a glorious and calm morning like this it takes some believing. Think about transporting livestock to

Trippers to
and from
the boat

and from Caldey in the autumn and winter, however, and you can see
why, for a while at least, market gardening and vegetable growing were
the prime industries of the place.

In the 19th century there was a successful quarrying
industry on Caldey: upwards of 20,000 tons of
limestone were exported each year. There were two lime
kilns here and boats regularly called at the island's jetty
to pick up the cargo.

These days about thirty people, apart from the monks,
live on Caldey all the year round. During the summer,
however, the population of the island is swelled by
hundreds of visitors each day. The place is also home to
thousands of sea birds: cormorants, gannets and gulls of
all description, who make their homes on the cliffs at the
south-western end of the island. If you are ever here at
evening, as we were last night, watch for the flocks of
birds heading for their nests on the precipitous cliff face.
For a while last night it seemed as if the sky was filled to
bursting with screaming seagulls. It was a spectacular
and awesome sight.

St Margaret's Island,
barely a dozen acres in
size, is just off the
western tip of Caldey
and many visitors to
the area do not even
know it's there. A
causeway used to
connect it to the larger
island and for a short
period in the 19th
century the place had a
thriving quarrying
industry with about 20
families living and
working here. These
days the island is
renowned for its
breeding colony of
cormorants, and there
is no public access.

The lighthouse on Caldey was built in 1828 by Trinity House. It stands high above Chapel Point on the south-east coast and was originally operated by three keepers. The light became fully automated in 1927.

By now I can hear people moving about on the deck below. It's time to go. Caldey is the one Welsh island that's relatively easy to access. Whilst it may be different from the others – it's certainly more lush, less rugged than most – it still has that magical quality to beguile and bewitch. As the smell of frying bacon begins to waft up the companionway, it's time to start the routine of the day.

5 MILFORD HAVEN

ON A LOVELY AFTERNOON of warm sunshine and gentle wind we set *Mascotte's* sails and prepare for the journey around the south Pembrokeshire coast. I spent my childhood here and the names on the chart are so familiar. Yet I've never seen any of these places from the sea or at such close quarters – Manorbier Castle peeping romantically through the cliffs, Barafundle Bay where we played and paddled every summer, Freshwater East where Uncle Frank had his dinghy and caravan.

St Govan's Chapel, ancient and eternally lonely, lies at the foot of its cliff, hidden from history's raiders. Freshwater West is the long and lovely beach where I used to go walking to blow away the cobwebs. Several chapters in my life are revisited in one short afternoon, on a single sea voyage, on a boat that is a century old.

The gunnery range patrol vessel intercepts us off Linney Head. The army has had a firing range here at Castlemartin and Merrion camp since the beginning of the Second World War. For many years in my childhood the ranges were used each summer by troops of the German Army. The Germans were welcome visitors in south Pembrokeshire but they stopped coming in the 1990s. These days the ranges are used mainly by British troops. The range vessel orders us to change course, our new route taking us some six miles out to sea, to avoid the firing.

St Govan's chapel

A turn at the tiller

From the deck of *Mascotte* we watch the puffs of white smoke as they rise high above the targets.

An hour before we arrive at the mouth of Milford Haven there comes a wail of deepest sorrow from somewhere off our starboard bow. It sounds like a man broken. And yet the ocean is empty, apart from *Mascotte*.

The noise comes again.

The wail unnerves even the oldest and most experienced aboard. It is

Stack Rock Fort   *photo* Mike Edmonds

The entrance to Milford Haven is guarded by several forts. One of them sits on Thorn Island, off the holiday village of Angle. This was the scene of a Welsh 'Whiskey Galore' when the *Loch Shiel* went ashore on the rocks of the island in 1894. The ship was carrying a cargo of whiskey and hundreds of locals spirited away the cargo before the coastguard could intervene. Stories abound of women carrying off bottles of spirits down the legs of their bloomers.

the sound an adult would make on learning that a deeply-felt fear has been realised or a terrible loss experienced. I stare at the horizon but there is nothing to be seen for miles around. Only when we draw near to the Haven's navigation buoy do we realise that this wave-propelled fog-horn sounds in all weathers. It has fooled us all.

The Heads of Milford Haven, as the opening to the estuary is called, heralds a hostile change in the weather. Suddenly there's stinging rain and cold wind, so sharp that no oilskins can ever keep them out. The lights of twinkling hamlets and villages on the twin banks of the narrow Haven look like a corridor of eyes watching our slow progress up stream – Angle, Herbrandston, Waterston and, eventually, Pembroke Dock.

For centuries, Britain's finest waited here for invasion. Napoleonic forts and towers were built across and around Milford Haven. Yet the soldiers and the military planners were disappointed. The enemy never came. The forts were there to protect mighty Pembroke Dockyard, once the premier ship-building yard in Britain. Hundreds of wooden-walls and pre-dreadnought battleships were built here, and five Royal Yachts.

The dockyard closed in 1926 but you can still see some of the old slipways and buildings at the western end of Pembroke Dock. In the twentieth century the oil industry joined the monuments of history, the refineries standing shoulder to shoulder along the banks of the Haven.

I remember coming down the Haven in a small boat, when we were

kids, when every refinery was firing and the waterway was thick with tankers. Each jetty presided majestically at the end of queuing metal hulls. Now the oil industry is rapidly joining the Napoleonic forts as a relic from a bygone age. When I was in school the fathers of at least half of my friends worked at one of the refineries or at Pembroke Power Station, now demolished. The oil refineries have been halved in number and I can't help wondering what those old school friends of mine are now doing for jobs.

By the time we pass Milford too many waves have crashed over *Mascotte* and we are all soaked, wet and quiet. There's a sterile hostility to a landscape of creaking tanker jetties and cold chimneys. Nobody in Pembrokeshire ever loved the oil industry for its beauty but, in its retreat, it resembles a fleeing husband leaving an uncomfortable marriage. Discarded shells of storage tanks and spaghetti pipelines scar the shores.

We arrive at Neyland marina by early evening. Dad used to bring me here when I was a small

Pembroke Dockyard was founded in 1814 and built over 200 warships for the Royal Navy. One of the most famous was *The Duke of Wellington* launched in 1852, the largest wooden battleship ever built. The town of Pembroke Dock grew quickly around the dockyard which, at its height, employed over 4000 men. The town remains as the only truly industrial community in Pembrokeshire.

Will
stows
the sails
as the
weather
changes

boy. Then the area was just a small, silted cove that nestled in under the flank of the Haven. Dad would walk me through the streets of Neyland, Brunel's shabby town, a place that had been long forgotten by great men.

'This place was meant to be the end of a great Trans-Atlantic trade route,' I say, more to myself than anyone in particular. 'You'd never believe it.'

Neyland Marina

Brunel's dream of a huge sea-port at the eastern end of Milford Haven came to nothing, although his famous liner, *The Great Eastern*, did lie here for several months, rotting away on a specially constructed grid and shutting out the light to the houses along the waterfront.

After years of depression, things are starting to improve and change in Neyland. There's a new marina, where we are to spend the night. I'm not sure what Brunel or my father would make of the place but I think they would be pleased to see the old town 'on the up' again.

Mascotte is an unwieldy ship. It's a bit like trying to park a truck in a multi-storey car park. The marina is built for trendy, agile yachts – not century-old cutters. The minutes spent manoeuvring begin to seem like hours. And all the time it gets colder and colder. When we finally tie up I can't feel the hot water in the marina's new shower block – I'm too cold.

Dinner in Neyland Sailing Club is a friendly affair and we sit surrounded by happy, smiling faces. Outside, the fiendish-looking night sky makes me relieved we are no longer in the Irish Sea. We spend most of the night drying our sodden clothes on *Mascotte's* boiling engine block, turning over the baked garments like pieces of toast on an open fire.

6   OUT TO SKOMER

WE CAST OFF AT FIRST LIGHT and ease down Milford Haven under the power of *Mascotte's* engine. Bacon sandwiches take some of the edge off the cold and rain. At the mouth of the Haven, some two hours out from Neyland, a school of dolphins swim off our bow and the day is transformed to sheer magic. Slowly we make our way to Skomer.

Soon we anchor off shore, gazing at one of the most famous, most romantic, of all Welsh islands. This is undoubtedly another Eden, Pembrokeshire's own earthly Paradise. Beneath the deafening cry of hundreds and thousands of puffins I row *Mascotte's* tender to the island's landing spot.

Skomer is the largest of the Pembrokeshire islands, over 720 acres and two miles long. It rises to a height of about 250 feet above sea level. One of the glories of Skomer is the wonderful array of wild flowers that adorn the island in the early summer. The fields of bluebells are stunning but the island also boasts thousands of primroses, red campion and thrift.

John Rogers, the artist, shows me around. We sit on a precarious ledge at the top of a high cliff while seals and dolphins play near the rocks below us. John comes here regularly to paint scenes of Skomer from his small boat. It's a life he wouldn't change.

'I ran away to the circus when I was young,' he says, grinning. 'I suppose it sounds very dramatic or even romantic, running away like

Filming seals

that. I worked as a rigger in the days when all of the circuses used the railway to travel around. Imagine the romance and action, packing all those animals and tents into the wagons? It was a great, grand adventure.'

John's father had once been shipwrecked on Flatholm Island, off Cardiff in the Bristol Channel. He survived to tell the tale – maybe that's why John loves islands so much. He has travelled around the world but has been drawn back to Pembrokeshire and Skomer to paint. I can see why.

My afternoon is spent with June Codd. She's the daughter of Reuben Codd, the last man to farm this island. He's a famous

John Rogers on the clifftop

'The Garland Stone, Skomer Island' (watercolour 19½ x 37½") by John Rogers.

character in Pembrokeshire, a man who was almost a legend in his own lifetime for his strength and bulldog tenacity. Trying to force a living from the soil of Skomer, Codd needed every last ounce of courage and determination.

June Codd and the ruins of the farmhouse where she grew up

When she was a child June was told that she had first been brought out to the island as a baby, lying in a wicker basket in a rowing boat. The times were rough and basic.

As a little girl June Codd spent all her holidays here. During term time she was packed off to boarding school in Fishguard. She's full of wonderful stories about growing up on Skomer.

'I used to milk the cows,' she tells me. 'We had four of them at that time and it was one of my jobs. I also used to free the rabbits that had been caught in the farm workers' traps – I don't know what the men would have said if they'd ever found out. I just couldn't bear to see the rabbits in pain, struggling to get free.'

June's curling, black and white photographs show the island's farmhouse in its prime. A big balcony ran the full length of the building's huge slate face. They had a grand piano in the parlour, June says. She is moved to tears when I ask her what she makes of the house now, ruined and empty.

'I suppose nature has reclaimed it, like it's reclaimed the rest of Skomer,' she shrugs, wiping her tears.

She's right. For centuries men battled against the elements here, but I suppose the result was inevitable. Nowadays there's no farming here, only birds and a handful of day visitors, each of them in search of a paradise that lies not too far away from home.

An old tractor from busier times

Skomer was farmed as far back as the Iron Age but it was with the coming of the Normans in the eleventh century that the place really found its purpose, as a warren for breeding and farming rabbits – rabbit flesh was something of a delicacy to the invaders. More traditional styles of farming were taken up in the eighteenth century. Now, in hindsight, it's amazing that farming survived for as long as it did on this windswept fist of rock. Standing here and staring at the rugged terrain, I marvel at the determination of the men and women who lived here for so many years.

Skomer Island, John Rogers' sketchbook

With my brothers Huw and Richard, and the Skomer goat

Skomer was named by the Viking raiders of the ninth and tenth centuries but evidence has been found of earlier habitation. The Harold Stone, a huge monolith that stands above the North Haven, is roughly similar to the standing stones of the Bronze Age.

These days the island is renowned for birds. Skomer's a nature reserve, run by the Wildlife Trust, South and West Wales, and is the place to come if you want to see puffins and Manx shearwaters. The birds burrow into the earth to make nests – it is the isolation of Skomer that has drawn them here. Birds who build their homes in the earth, on the ground, are easy prey to predators like rats and foxes. So the remoteness and isolation of places like Skomer – and the tiny Midland Isle which lies a few hundred yards away from the main island – offer a natural habitat for puffins and shearwaters.

Path to the ruined farmstead

Late that afternoon, as I row the tender back to *Mascotte*, the thought of nearby Jack Sound is not particularly comforting. The Sound is a wild tide race that separates Skomer from the mainland and it's just a few hundred yards beyond the looming hull of *Mascotte*. Only the very foolish, or perhaps the very skilled, would try to take on the Sound in a small boat like this – I'm neither of those but the thought of somehow missing the painter which hangs over the side of *Mascotte* and being swept out into that raging torrent is something that fills me with dread. Reuben Codd and the other farmers had to face the terrors of the Sound many times, in all weathers.

Puffins

The sea around Skomer has been designated a Marine Nature Reserve, the first of its kind in Britain. Yet it's the memory of the island's birds that I'll take away with me, the puffins and guillemots. I would have liked to have said it was the shearwaters that I will remember but they are nocturnal birds, only returning to the island when night falls. You need to stay over if you wish to see and, more memorably, hear them.

Skomer, along with Skokholm, Grassholm and Midland islands, is home to about 150,000 pairs of Manx shearwaters. It remains the world's largest population of breeding pairs.

EXPEDITION SKOMER

A boast of boys and a giggle of girls
in a boat off the higgledy piggledy coast
that wriggles through caves and coves and curls

to the waves of the holy bay of Saint Bride:
a boat that, preserves of nature, behaves
like a sliding, unstrapped saddle astride

the bottle-green, battle-bright hogsback sea.
So we rear our rocking-horse way across
from the wracks of Wales to the black bohea

of the bay of Skomer, the sea-green dome
of the pirate island with the cruel Norse name
where seals and smugglers have felt at home,

and Look! (shout the children) A puffin – there!
as we shrug round another shoulder of stone
and the sound of the outboard stutter and swear

at our heel splutters out, and the silken sand –
saffron and smooth – slides under the keel.
Then, praising God, I land.

Raymond Garlick

7   TO RAMSEY

SKOMER ISLAND DISAPPEARING rapidly behind us, we sail towards Ramsey across St Bride's Bay, past the yellow streak of Musselwick Sands. Nab Head, Stack Rocks, Little Haven, Broad Haven, Settling Nose, Druidstone Haven and Solva all pass by to starboard. The Preseli Mountains rise up on the distant horizon, then Ramsey Island suddenly appears ahead of us below *Mascotte's* mainsail.

The island was once heavily cultivated, far more than Skomer and perhaps even as much as Caldey. As soon as you land and climb up to the clifftop you begin to pick out a network of stone walls – old boundary markers – criss-crossing the land. It's amazing, now, to stand on Ramsey and think about the lives of all the farmers who once tried to earn a crust out here. There must have been easier ways of earning a living.

Today, Phil 'Ramsey' Davies has returned to Ramsey to join us. He first came to the island in the 1950s, after losing both his wife and daughter to TB. I cannot think of a more desolate place to grieve than this beautiful but remote island. Yet this was certainly a place of healing for Phil.

Even now, in his 80s, Phil Davies exudes the energy that must have kept him going out here, some fifty years ago.

'Even in my time here,' he says, 'the island was farmed pretty

Approaching Ramsey

Looking back at mainland Pembrokeshire

extensively. Just ignore the sea around you, if that's possible, and think about the terrain. As far as the land is concerned you could be standing in any farmyard or pasture in Wales. Until you stare at the ground.'

He's right. Where you'd expect soft earth, hard rock twists your ankles. The grass is mostly hollowed out, home to thousands of rabbits. Making a living from this volcanic outcrop must have been a Herculean task.

If Phil had fled from tragedy on the mainland, disaster still stalked him on Ramsey. Three of his friends were drowned in a boating accident that nearly claimed him too.

'I was lucky,' he shrugs. 'I guess it just wasn't my time.'

I've never met anyone who's almost died but I imagine that a brush with death like that will determine your perspective for the rest of your life – probably more than anything you'll ever encounter.

As we walk around the deserted farm and its rusting implements, Phil says there was never any time to feel lonely out here. There were always too many cows to milk or fields to tend or fish to catch. Without anyone to help him, he was fully occupied in trying to survive on one of the most difficult farms in Wales.

Phil lives on the mainland now. The island he farmed has become home to wild animals, his fields given over to the frolicking of hundreds of rabbits. The humans who, for so many generations, made this place their home have long since accepted nature's will. There are only visitors now, like many of the migratory birds – here with the spring, gone by autumn.

Phil as a young man on Ramsey

On the afternoon tourist boat from St Justinian on the mainland come Harold Copsey and Melba Griffiths. They struggle up the harbour slope along with a dozen other visitors.

'I was evacuated from wartime London,' says Harold, 'to avoid the bombing, and found myself sent out here as a farm boy. This is the first time I've been back in sixty years.'

One of Harold's most significant memories is of the luggage tag that was fastened to his coat as he stood on Paddington Station. Then came the long train journey across Britain to Haverfordwest. It went on for hours, he tells me – and that was before the trip to Ramsey. Life on the island was radically different from the East End of

Known in Welsh as Ynys Dewi, Ramsey Island takes its English name from the old Norse language – it was called Hfran-ey. The island has two hills, Carn Llundain and Carn Ysgubor, reaching 446 ft and 323 ft respectively. Both of them have pre-historic burial chambers on top.

Harold with director Sara Allen

London but he soon found himself taking charge of the animals. Milking, collecting eggs and tending to the pigs became his daily routine. Now, quietly, he admits to once losing a piglet over the cliff edge in a moment of distraction. What the farmer thought about the accident he doesn't say.

Although they have travelled to Ramsey today on the same boat, Harold hasn't met Melba Griffiths yet. She is the widow of Elfed Griffiths, who died recently. Elfed was the son of the man who farmed Ramsey in the 1940s, before Phil Davies took over. Harold used to look after the young Elfed when he was just a young child.

Melba has brought photograph albums with her, hundreds of grainy black and

There are many legends and stories about St Justinian who, allegedly, lived on Ramsey. One states that he was very strict and rigid with his followers. In despair, they rebelled and cut off his head. Undismayed, the saint simply picked up his severed head and walked across Ramsey Sound until he came to the spot where his chapel now stands. There he died and was buried. The rebellious followers soon died from unspecified but hideously painful diseases.

white snaps. The Illustrated London News visited Ramsey in the 1940s and shot dozens of portraits and landscape views for the magazine. I introduce Melba to Harold and she weeps.

'I had the happiest years of my life with Elfed and I miss him so much,' she sighs, staring at Harold. 'He'd have loved to meet you. Now it's all too late.'

We spend several hours eavesdropping on the conversation between two people who eagerly exchange stories about a man who is clearly much missed.

Harold and Melba share memories

Harold tells us that although there was only a handful of people living on Ramsey, the farmer and his family always lived and ate separately from the workers. Even in Paradise, it seems, some were more equal than others, particularly in 1940s Britain.

A walk to the summit

In the afternoon I walk to the summit of Ramsey, passing rabbits and a small herd of deer. From the top of the island, on a beautiful and sunny day like this, you feel as if you can almost touch the mainland. There is a patchwork cloth of green, brown and purple heather, then shades of deep blue, before your eyes are assaulted by the yellows and reds of Pembrokeshire's fields on the mainland.

In the evening, one of the St Justinian speedboats races us around Ramsey's caves. There are scores of them. A little girl asks her mother if there are magic dragons living here. I want her mother to say yes, and I want to believe her.

Evening motor boat trip from St Justinian's

8 FROM RAMSEY TO FISHGUARD

SHELTERING FROM the morning's torrential rain in the old lifeboat house at St Justinian's, we meet RNLI coxswain Malcolm Grey. Walrus-like, peering over his moustache and glasses, he stares out towards foaming Ramsey Sound. His grandfather was coxswain here and, before that, had been yet another of Ramsey's tenant farmers. He sold rabbits to pay the rent.

We gaze out to the island, no more than a mile away from the mainland. Yet on a day like this it might as well be on the moon. No boatman will be crossing the Bitches today. These jagged stumps of rock protrude like broken teeth from the waters of the Sound. According to local legend, the Bitches are all that's left of a causeway that once connected Ramsey to the mainland. The bad-tempered St Justinian is supposed to have smashed down the causeway to gain himself a little privacy on the island.

Legend apart, the Bitches have been the cause of many disasters. One of the most famous was in 1910, when the St Davids lifeboat, *Gem*, was wrecked here while carrying out a rescue in the Sound. Coxswain John Stephens and two of his crewmen were drowned, the survivors having to spend a wet, cold and terrifying night clinging to the Bitches before help could reach them the next day. It is a tale of courage and tragedy, qualities that lifeboat-men and all sailors know only too well.

The Bitches
photo Nona Rees

Before the days of VHF radio Ramsey islanders would build a bonfire on the cliffs if they needed help or wanted to attract the attention of people on the mainland. It would be a brave man who sailed out there today, whoever needed help. The tide is racing through the Sound at speeds that must reach 6 or 7 knots.

'The St Davids lifeboat used to be kept a couple of miles away, in the middle of the town,' Malcolm tells me. 'It was sat up on rollers, covered by a huge canvas tarpaulin in the Square. Then the Cathedral clerics got a bit worried by the activities of courting couples – well, it was an open invitation, I suppose – under the canvas!'

After the complaints from the Cathedral the boat was moved out of St Davids and installed on the gentler waters of Ramsey Sound at St Justinian.

We make for Fishguard. The force 5 has turned into force 7 and *Mascotte* lurches and crashes from one roller to the next. Crockery smashes below in the saloon. There's a fine line between exhilaration and fear and we've just crossed it. The radio chants a litany of small craft in trouble around the coast – maydays in the distance. Then comes the chatter of the lifeboat VHF trying to locate them. Everyone's silent, hoping that the talk between strangers doesn't end.

The Smalls is a series of half-submerged rocks, constantly swept by storms and the tide, lying about 20 miles out in the Atlantic. A lighthouse was built on the rocks but in 1800 one of the two keepers died. The weather was dreadful and, not knowing what else to do, the surviving keeper made a rough coffin, and lashed his companion's body to the rail of the lighthouse. It was several weeks before relief reached the Smalls and, by then, the lighthouse keeper had gone insane. Trinity House later insisted on all its lights being manned by three keepers.

On deck with Will – a few stages before exhilaration turned to fear

Strumble Head

The rugged rocks of the Bishops and Clerks stand out menacingly behind us as we pass St Davids Head. Abereiddy, Porth-gain and Abercastle are named on our navigation chart but today there's only grey sea blurring with an even greyer sky. Strumble Head rears and teases us in the distance. There are still hours to go.

By the time we make Fishguard, *Mascotte* has tipped and swayed with the savage sea far too often for enjoyment. Even in the haven of the harbour the swell is too great to tie up to the wall. We anchor out in the bay instead. It isn't long before the harbour master moves us, to make way for the late Irish ferry's manoeuvres planned for midnight, tide and weather permitting.

A number of rocks and islets lie off Ramsey. These include Ynyscantwr (the Enchanter's Isle) and Ynys Bery (the Falcon's Isle). The islets are now inaccessible but many years ago sheep were sometimes herded and grazed on Ynys Bery.

Soaked and cold, we wash in *Mascotte's* basins and change for a night in town. We take the tender to the harbour slip and our dry clothes are quickly soaked by the angry swell and spray. I remember Tony Winter's words about sailing accidents in tenders like this one and, for a while, we come perilously close to adding to the list.

It's dinner, then last orders in *The Royal Oak* where the French signed the peace agreement after the last invasion of Britain two hundred years ago. A dozen instrumentalists pack the pub tonight, playing the most wonderful music.

'No casualties after all the Mayday calls today,' announces Fishguard's lifeboat coxswain as he joins us at the bar. That's good news. Then he plays his guitar.

Back on the slipway there's a clear sky. The stars are shining and I can see the Plough. I am suddenly seven years old again, standing on the pavement in Victoria Street, Pembroke Dock, and staring up at the sky with my dad. We never did get much beyond the Plough. It was always too cold. In *Mascotte's* cramped bunk, rolling (with or without the harbour swell) I fall asleep, exhausted and drunk.

Fishguard was the scene of the last invasion of Britain when, in 1797, a force of 1400 Frenchmen landed on Carreg Wastad Point to the west of the town. The invasion lasted barely three days and was a farcical affair worthy of *Dad's Army*. Yet it did lead to panic in the country, a run on the banks and the Bank of England having to issue the first pound note in British history.

9 BEARING NORTH

IT'S BRIGHT SKIES and calm seas for early anchor weighing at Fishguard harbour, then off on a bearing north towards Bardsey. It's difficult to imagine that this is the same stretch of water as yesterday's boiling sea. The ocean is ours and is completely empty. We see no one except for a distant yacht, several miles away.

Father and son setting sail

We have an eight-hour sail ahead of us. We cruise past Dinas Head and the foothills of the distant Cambrian Mountains loom on the far horizon. Cardigan Island appears off our starboard bow. Now a nature reserve, the island was the scene of a famous shipwreck in 1934. The old liner *Herefordshire* was being towed to the Clyde for scrapping when she broke free from her tugs and piled up on the rocks of the island. Rats from the old ship escaped onto the shore and established a huge colony which proceeded to demolish all the wildlife. They lived on Cardigan Island until 1968 when they were killed off by warfarin experiments.

In full sail

After Fishguard the west coast of Wales has no deep water ports, places that could welcome a vessel with *Mascotte's* ten-foot draft. If the weather turns bad again a smaller boat could run for cover in New Quay, Aberaeron or Barmouth but not this pilot cutter. She was made for deep water ports and harbours. So Aberystwyth and Aberdovey are places we pass, too far to starboard to identify or observe.

This morning Tony Winter takes *Mascotte's* helm. He used to be a ship owner who ran coasters around the shores of Britain.

'Sailing's in the blood,' he says. 'I learnt the ropes with my father on the east coast of England. Years later I bought and restored the *Mascotte* for racing. At least, that was the general idea.'

If I was ever a rich man I'm not sure that fighting with the tiller of a hundred-year-old hulk in the wilds of the Irish Sea would be my favourite pastime. But it is Tony's. When we're not sailing he is polishing and cleaning, mending and checking. He wants *Mascotte* to look her best when the helicopter arrives to film aerial shots for the TV film we are making. If he polishes the brightwork any more, he'll blind the pilot.

Will serving culinary miracles.

Tony's son Will is a former banker who's jacked in his job in the city. He's taking time out to think about life: in a few months, he's going to be married. Our sail around the coast of Wales is punctuated by daily progress reports on preparations for the coming nuptials. Like his father, Will is half man, half fish. He's grown up on the sea. He's the first mate on *Mascotte*. He sets the sails, fishes for supper on long lines off the back of the boat and then cooks for us. He does all the hard work – and on a boat without much modern equipment there is a lot of hard work to do. Will's cheerfulness, even when faced by storms of gale force eight, is comforting and reassuring. Cooking for seven people in a galley the size of a small cupboard, when everything around is constantly moving, is something I'll admire all the more, having tried it myself several times on this journey.

St Tudwal's East and West are two islands off Abersoch on the Llŷn Peninsula. The largest of the pair (St Tudwal's East) covers 26 acres and has evidence of habitation dating from the Roman era. The name St Tudwal derives from Bishop Tugdual who fled to Wales from Brittany following the collapse of the Roman Empire in the 6th century.

In *Mascotte's* heyday she'd have been manned by just two people, but on our journey, with all the requirements of a television crew, we need a little more help. Neither Tony nor Will has sailed right around the coast of Wales but John Hart and his wife Margaret are veterans. They act as pilot and navigator. John used to be a harbour pilot and was once coxswain of the Barry lifeboat. These days he's the Royal Yachting Association's examiner and, just for good measure, also skippers super yachts for the super rich. He and Margaret run a sailing school in Spain. Between them they offer the best local knowledge and the finest sailing skills. They are also a mine of fascinating stories that keep us going when land disappears and there is nothing ahead of us but blue and the compass.

'It's beautiful out here,' I say, 'but it must get lonely at times.'

John nods.

'It's OK now, when you guys are here. But if you're on your own, yes it can be very lonely.'

John gives off an air of total confidence, a wise man totally in his element out here with the sea.

'Any sailor who heads north from the Bristol Channel – on a regular basis – has to know this coastline pretty well. I've delivered boats to lots of places along here –

Margaret Hart, setting sail

yachts, lifeboats, all types of vessels. So you could say I know it as well as anyone.'

'You must have some great stories about the sea, about this area.'

He laughs but he's not going to be drawn. Not yet.

'Sure,' he says. 'I've got some great stories. But it's always nicer talking about them afterwards – when we anchor at Bardsey, say, for a cup of tea or a meal. There's always the danger of things changing so quickly when you're out at sea.'

Jon Rees, cameraman

I know what he means. Within minutes the weather can range from calm to raging fury, then back again.

Our camera man is Jon Rees, a friend I've worked with since starting in television. He hangs over the side of *Mascotte*, dangling his camera in the water to gain shots that have the rest of us scared. It's the type of thing directors love.

Camera crews are famed for their life of comfortable hotels and glamorous locations. Watching Jon work, in clothes that are constantly soaked, for days on end, he must wish he'd turned down this job to

In full sail, bound for north Wales

spend more time with his new baby. Then the sun comes out and shines on *Mascotte's* sails – old cream squares pitched against a sky and sea of pure blue. We could be heading for Treasure Island, except that it's freezing cold. You wouldn't find Long John Silver in these waters. His cutlass would rust, even in the summer.

At dusk we draw close to Bardsey. You can't mistake the lopsided, hump-backed shape of the place. However, the island boat to the mainland has been cancelled – it's too rough to land. We quickly come to the same conclusion. *Mascotte* will run the risk of being battered by the sea and wind if we anchor here tonight. We're short on fuel, fresh water and food. Tony, John and Margaret weigh up the implications of a frantic

The island – as it might have been if weather had been kinder

South Stack

night of anchor watch or making for Holyhead and returning to Bardsey by sailing around Anglesey over the next few days.

There really is no choice. Bardsey disappears into the distance and we set a course for Holyhead. In this wind, in these seas, it's some five hours sailing across Caernarfon Bay. Off to starboard lie Caernarfon Bar and the Menai Straits – our return route when we make the trip back to Bardsey.

At a quarter to ten, on the north-west coast of Anglesey, South Stack is abeam. Then comes North Stack. Finally, we round the port's vast breakwater – the wall that shelters both the port and the new marina – and sail into calmer waters. *Mascotte* would have been a regular visitor here some 90 years ago, touting for trade from the Liverpool ships bound for south Wales ports. We bump awkwardly onto the modern landing stage, made for sleeker, more agile vessels, not this ship from another age, from another world.

Two small islands to the east of Aberdaron Bay are Ynys Gwylan Fawr and Ynys Gwylan Fach. With a combined area of just 20 acres, they are sometimes known as the Gull Islands.

Holyhead is renowned as a ferry port, one of the main landing and departure points for Irish trade. Most visitors don't realise the port and town sit on a separate island from Anglesey – Holy Island. These days a wide causeway links it to Anglesey. You never realise that when you drive to the port you are crossing from one island to another.

The first packet boats to Ireland began to sail out of Holyhead in the 1570s but it was the coming of the railway in the Victorian age that brought real prosperity to the area. It's good to see that its usefulness and status as a port has continued into the twenty-first century.

We turn in for the night. Tomorrow we begin our sail around Anglesey, wind and tide permitting.

Stena ferry at Holyhead

10 SAILING AROUND ANGLESEY

JEFF GARROD, ARCHITECT for Holyhead's marina, proudly shows me his grand plans for expansion. This place is set for development and now that the road across the island has been improved, access to and from the port has been made much easier. We sit in Jeff's office and gaze at the future.

In the background the Irish ferries and catamarans from Dublin and Dun Laoghaire ignore the strong winds and tides to deliver and collect their passengers. Further along the coast Michael O'Rourke, the duty coastguard, whiskered like Father Christmas, listens unnoticed to Anglesey's sailors gossiping on their radios. Errant teenagers call 'Coastguard, Coastguard'. The messages are invariably followed by a father's embarrassed and profuse apologies. A tired rebuke is returned from the harbour.

Designing the marina

We wait for the turn of the tide. At last, *Mascotte* eases out of Holyhead's bitter harbour. The sun peaks out of the clouds to tease our freezing fingers and faces as we sail past the Skerries lighthouse, past the Platters, West Mouse and Middle Mouse.

Holyhead's two great institutions – ferry to Ireland and the lifeboat

On the shore a chapel and graveyard cling to the rocks, a sad memorial to lost mariners. The *Royal Charter* was wrecked here in 1859, in a storm still known as 'The Royal Charter Gale'. Over 400 people were drowned, many of them prosperous prospectors who were returning from Australia laden with gold and silver. Ironically, after such far-flung adventures, they lost their lives within a few hundred yards of the shore. Watchers and would-be rescuers stood helplessly on the cliffs and shoreline, unable to help in any way. Charles Dickens came to Anglesey to write about the shipwreck which is, perhaps, the most famous of all the many disasters off the Welsh coast.

We're heading for the port of Amlwch. It's remote and hidden from the sea but as we round the headland and East Mouse islet, it becomes a sizable port. *Mascotte* nuzzles in between *My Rose Anne*,

Resting-place for many of those who lost their lives at sea

Cariad and *The Gilsea*, rust-streaked hulks that are now resting after a night's fishing. The crews empty their cargoes of scallops, shellfish that are eventually bound for Spain. Dogfish are thrown aside on the harbour wall, reeking bait for tomorrow's catch.

Amlwch harbour

Lunar landscape of Paris copper mine, which once made Amlwch a thriving port

Thomas Telford's suspension bridge.

Amlwch is one of the most romantic ports we've yet visited; it grew around the export of copper. The shipbuilders constructed their vessels on the hill, before sliding them into the bay. Today's pilot boats tie up here, waiting to guide ships into Liverpool. Orange, sleek and shiny, the pilot boats are state-of-the-art vessels, just like *Mascotte* would have been in her day.

The skipper of *The Gilsea* gives us a basket of plaice and Dover sole, enough to keep us going for days and we head out towards Menai Bridge. It's still freezing cold but strong winds make for wonderful sailing. We fly past Moelfre, Benllech, Puffin Island and Gallows Point. At Beaumaris lies what is surely the most perfect concentric castle ever built, the supreme example of the medieval castle builder's art. First established in 1298, the fortress was developed over hundreds of years and was never truly completed. Yet the shell of the building remains, a lasting tribute to the stonemason's skills, speaking loudly still of subjugation and defensiveness.

Britannia Bridge: another impressive structure

We tie up at a jetty close to the Menai Bridge and sit down to a feast of fresh fish. Anglesey used to be known as Môn, Mam Cymru – Anglesey, Mother of Wales – as the island was once a huge granary, supplying corn to all parts of the country. It was also renowned for its cows. At one time over 3000 head of cattle were swum across the Menai Straits each year by the famous drovers of Wales – shades of *Rawhide*. Now you can cross the Straits on one of two bridges. Thomas Telford's magnificent suspension bridge was built in 1826. The construction cost of £120,000 possibly seemed a lot of money then.

At first light we're off, through the Swellies, which we take at high water. We sail under the suspension bridge, then the Britannia railway (and road) bridge and head towards Port Dinorwic. We carefully negotiate the old lock into the new marina, just one of many developments springing up all around the coast of Wales.

Anglesey has 124 miles of coastline and several smaller islands lie just off shore. These include Ynys Meibion, Ynys Dulas and Puffin Island. The Menai Straits has many islands, places like Church Island, Ynys Gorad Goch, the Swellies and Ynys Welltog. Most, if not all of these islands, are now uninhabited. There are also many dangerous rocks around the coast, such as Harry Furlough's Reef, which have claimed the lives of many sailors over the centuries.

The helicopter filming *Mascotte*

Out there, in the Straits, is Ynys Gorad Goch – Whitebait Island as it used to be called. From 1820 until well into the twentieth century the Madoc Jones family lived on the island, making their living selling whitebait teas to tourists and passing yachtsmen – hence the name. Ynys Gorad Goch is just one of many small islands in the Menai Straits.

We are due to meet the artist Sir Kyffin Williams who lives on the banks of the Straits. *Mascotte's* tender takes us to shore. Shoes and socks off, trousers rolled up, we all limp across the sharp stones and shingle of the beach. Kyffin has forgotten we were coming; not that you'd know it. He greets us like long lost friends. His cottage is full of fine paintings and sculptures, and centuries-old Welsh furniture. The backdrop to the house is a canvas of the wonderful Menai Bridge. It's an epic setting to meet one of the living legends of Wales.

As we walk on the foreshore, Kyffin tells me of his forebears who founded an early lifeboat on Anglesey. He's greatly taken with our pilot, John Hart, who is himself a former lifeboat coxswain. For a man in his golden years Kyffin is the best television interviewee I've ever come across. He understands the medium better than most professionals. Each

Talking to Sir Kyffin Williams

time I restart the interview, at a different angle in his garden, he recaps all the highlights of our previous questions and answers. The film editor will love him.

'Island people are aloof,' Kyffin says and chuckles. 'They can't help it; it's the way they are.'

He makes mischief with his eyes. Then, with a wiggle of his

70

'Sun over the Bay, Llanddwyn' (24 x 24 ins) by Kyffin Williams

walrus moustache, he's off onto another subject before we can fully explore the first one. He loves and hates the Menai Straits – they are his muse and also the flooding wrecker of his home. We cross a low board pinned to the bottom of the frame on his front door. It is a feeble obstacle to summer's high tides. Kyffin shows off his garden, full of plants and sculptures. His commentary on the shrubbery is interspersed with several broadsides against the arts establishment. I tell him about our trip around Wales.

'Painting the sea is an autobiographical process,' he says. 'The paintings are all about the artist, not the scenery.'

Passing Plas Newydd, the home of the Marquis of Anglesey

Kyffin Williams is a wonderful raconteur. He recalls a tale of saving his neighbours' boats during a violent storm by lassoing the vessels to a tree. His neighbours rewarded his kindness by later dropping a mackerel wrapped in newspaper through his letterbox. Unfortunately he had just left for a two-week holiday.

Kyffin comes down to the shore to see us off, his barefooted, unexpected visitors. We wade out to the tender, shoes and socks in hand. He waves with both his hands high above his head. I'd expected a legend and he didn't disappoint.

11 RETURN TO BARDSEY

THE SANDBANKS of Caernarfon Bar cause some concern aboard *Mascotte* on our journey out of the Menai Straits. On a vessel with no echo sounder and no way of checking the depth other than the age-old process of swinging the lead – dropping a heavy weight attached to a line over the bows – local knowledge is crucial in order to ensure a safe passage.

John Hart and Tony Winter do a wonderful job of negotiating the shifting sands. It is a dramatic few hours of great judgement, at the right stage of the tide, all set against the most wonderful scenery that north Wales has to offer. Bearings are taken on Abermenai Point and Llanddwyn Island. The navigation chart warns of the wreck of the *Grampian Castle* and advises caution to all mariners. We skirt the area carefully, not wanting to end up as another wreck on the chart.

Caernarfon Castle looks even more spectacular from the water. At least I'm told that it does by the hungry crew members who are waiting for me to produce a cooked breakfast from the galley. True to its era, *Mascotte* has a paraffin cooker. The smell of the fuel, combined with the motion of the boat, nearly provides the waiting diners with a little extra helping on top of their plates of bacon, Spam, sausage and egg. Yes, I did say Spam. Yes, they do still make it. We leave Caernarfon Bar at

10.45 and a south-westerly wind, force 4 to 5, blows us to Bardsey Sound by 15.30.

Bardsey lies only a few miles off the tip of the Llŷn Peninsula. It's named after the Norse warrior Bardr, and in Welsh it is called Ynys Enlli – the island of the tide race. It's well named, as we found to our cost

Mascotte approaching the island – to land this time

when we first tried to land here. According to one strand of Arthurian legend Bardsey was the home of Merlin the Magician and the sense of remoteness about the place makes you think that there could be more than a little truth to the story.

The island seems to be a busy place, its jetty a hive of activity this afternoon. Sharing the bay with *Mascotte* are a couple of fishing boats and the launch from Aberdaron bringing and collecting day trippers and supplies. The Aberdaron boat is low in the water, heavy with thirty or so eager birdwatchers, naturalists and escapees from the mainland. The boxes and packages on the boat's deck are wrapped in plastic to shield the groceries from the worst of the spray.

The jetty is made of rocks bound with wire netting. We're met by a line of passengers heading back to Aberdaron, clad in colourful waterproofs, looking like penguins on parade. Luggage and people move off the boat to be replaced by the eager, waiting throng. There's no pushing or shoving as there would be on the Underground. These people are, for the most part, birdwatchers and they just don't do that sort of thing. Besides, their binoculars might get damaged.

'I walked for two miles or so uphill to get a view of Bardsey Island . . . Sheep graze on the heathery moorland and, four miles off in the sea, is an island like a huge mouse. Bardsey is a gentle, dome-shaped hill with a long tail of flat land flung out behind it.'
H V Morton *In Search of Wales*. 1932

An ancient tractor and trailer wait for us to load our overnight bags before slowly inching its way over the unmade stone tracks. Regular visitors and children hitch a lift. Within seconds the thirty passengers on the jetty disappear across the island. Some are studying seals, others birds. Many, like me, have just come to see what's happening here at the end of Wales.

In the middle of a pile of suitcases, soft bags and small children, Mick Lipscombe, the island's manager, is loading luggage. He looks exactly like an islander should look – wild, thin, with a windswept greying

Waving off the visitors who are leaving for Aberdaron on the mainland

Mynydd Enlli, known simply as the Mountain

beard. He's only been here for a year. I ask him what he misses most about the mainland.

'Nothing really,' he shrugs. 'I've got my family out here with me. I can't say I need anything else.'

Each time I meet an islander – and it doesn't matter which island I'm on – I can't help thinking they're running away from something. And yet, at the same time, they always exude such a sense of calm that maybe, just maybe, they've actually been able to find what they've been looking for.

Chris Arnold, the chairman of Bardsey Island Trust, is an archaeologist. He takes me to a ruined stone farmhouse that he's excavated. The floor is lower than you'd expect, tons of soil having been removed during the excavation.

'Dig anywhere on this island,' Chris says, 'and you'll soon find human bones. There were settlements on Bardsey thousands of years ago, so human remains are in plentiful supply.'

He shows me an ancient grave, now exposed and open to the elements by the steady and relentless traffic of footsteps on the path.

'I was sitting here once and rested my hand on the ground,' Chris explains. 'The next second I had pushed right through a brittle skull that was lying just below the surface of the earth.'

Great, I think, that should really help me to sleep tonight. Twenty thousand saints, they say, have been buried on Bardsey. Whether or not that's true I really don't know. What I do know, however, is that in the Middle Ages this was a place of pilgrimage. Three visits here equalled one trip to Rome. So the island does seem to have been regularly visited by people seeking saintliness or redemption.

Ian Jolly is a retired British Telecom engineer. We meet him as we walk. Bardsey is the kind of place where total strangers stop to talk to you in the middle of the road. Ian is fitting Bardsey with its first telephone exchange. It's a party line system with lots of wind-up phones, just like the ones you see in old Hollywood films, with Humphrey Bogart or Edward G Robinson. Soon all the cottages will be connected. Each phone has a unique ring tone but anyone could answer the call. The equipment was made in Britain in the 1930s, shipped out to New Zealand and then used there. It's been recently bought on the internet and sent over to

Bardsey is burial-place for twenty thousand saints

Cottages on Bardsey see a flow of visitors who are keen to experience island life

Bardsey. Only a wind-up system like this will work here, Ian tells us, because of the paucity of power.

I'm staying in the island's farmhouse as the guest of David and Libby Barnden. As soon as I arrive there's a crisis. David has been told by one of the day-trippers that there is a sheep with blood running down its face, in urgent need of attention. The only trouble is, he can't quite remember where the beast is located.

'This is the best and worst place in Wales to farm,' David says. 'You have hundreds of pairs of eyes watching over your livestock. Yet everybody always gives you a different location for the problem or the casualty.'

I leave my luggage and join David in his search for the missing bloody lamb. We soon find it, further up the island's only track, past fields and cottages, beyond the chapel. The lamb has caught one of its erupting horns and made it bleed profusely. There's no vet to call out here, no James Herriot to rush to your aid. After chasing the lamb unsuccessfully around the field for several minutes, we finally manage to usher it back to the farmyard where David covers the damaged horn with antiseptic.

'You should see my bedside table,' he says. 'With all the books I've got it looks like a cross between a reading list for a medical student and a vet. I still don't know which one is most useful.'

On the other side of the stone farmyard a couple of large pigs – Dyson and Hoover – are enjoying the afternoon sunshine. David says they recently grew tired of two chickens who were constantly eating their food. So the pigs ate the chickens. I've never given a great deal of thought to what pigs ate until now. I'm reminded of it again when, next morning, our director Sara Allen can't

> Following the Battle of Chester in the sixth century over a thousand monks escaped the slaughter and took refuge on Bardsey. This may be the basis of the legend of Bardsey's saints.

David Barnden

finish her ample cooked breakfast of bacon and eggs. The left-over meal is put into the swill bin for the pigs to eat. Cannibalism – on Bardsey.

Libby Barnden produces a large tin bowl and starts to milk the three goats that provide all the yoghurt and milk for the island. Her children suddenly appear and finish the job. The children have missed a year's

Libby Barnden with her goats

schooling to be out here on Bardsey. At first I wonder what they'll have missed of the National Curriculum. By the time I leave the island, I envy their time spent learning to look after animals and studying the seals and birds alongside some of the world's greatest scientists. Perhaps even more important, they have been spending part of their formative years communing with nature. Far removed from things the mainland deems to be important, theirs is a world that is governed by tides and the weather, where learning to talk to people from all walks of life is important – not the latest video game.

There is to be a barbecue on the beach on Saturday night, the highlight of Bardsey's social calendar. Yesterday's yachts make today's

Playing on the beach, Cafn Enlli

timber for the bonfire. Each islander has cooked food – and a lot of it seems to be lamb! Some seventy people are expected. David and Libby's Aga is going full pelt, roasting a joint and baking bread, enough to feed an army. Their home reminds me of my grandmother's kitchen. Even in blazing sunshine her stove was always full on, the only method of providing hot water and cooking at the same time.

The morning after the beach party, and the barbecue fire still burns

The islanders have built the bonfire on the windward side of the island. It doesn't take us long to realise that as the sun sets we'll all be chilled to the bone in the biting winds. So, plank by plank, with the help of the tractor and trailer, the fire is re-sited on the lee shore beach, below a low-lying cliff, out of the wind. Islanders come with food and drink, then sit talking in front of the flames on a beach washed by the beam of the lighthouse and by the gentle waves from the bay. I've never been to a party before where the largest family is the seals that are lying just off shore.

The barbecue lasts into the small hours. I make my way back along the track to the farmhouse, the full moon lighting the path and its gates. For an island paradise Bardsey is a noisy place at night. The bark of seals, the chatter of birdsong and the bleating of restless lambs chorus me to bed.

When I arrive back at the farmhouse I realise I've forgotten to bring a candle. I stumble over most of the furniture in the darkness. There are no electric lights and my attempts to find switches on the walls are pointless.

I am woken in the morning by an enthusiastic cockerel. Through the window I can see the bonfire on the beach, still well alight. Like all the houses on Bardsey the farmhouse has a compost toilet, one that uses a sprinkling of sawdust rather than water after use. I have to admit that, after a heavy night, it is an interesting introduction to sustainable living.

Many Welsh islands once had religious settlements. The rugged and isolated life on these windswept islands appealed to the early religious martyrs. Puffin Island (off Anglesey), Bardsey, Caldey and Ramsey all hosted religious cells but so, too, did tiny islets like St Tudwals near Abersoch and Gateholm in Pembrokeshire.

Ernest Evans ready to motor out to check lobster pots

In a small fishing boat tied up at the jetty, Ernest Evans is getting ready to check his pots for lobster and crab, just like his father and grandfather have done before him.

'I've always been a bit of a loner,' he says. 'I like island life and I like Bardsey. Its mountain feels like it's somebody's back, turned against the mainland. I like that.'

We motor out of the bay and haul two pots from the seabed. Their buoys are nearly flooded by the rising tide but the wire cages each hold a couple of lobsters and crabs. Ernest measures them and throws back an undersized but grateful crab. The lobsters are a beautiful porcelain blue.

'Lobsters come in lots of different shades,' Ernest says, 'depending on which part of the coast you're on. These shellfish will be sold to a wholesaler on Anglesey.'

We wonder why the British don't like spider crabs, yet the French and Spanish can't get enough of them, all from our shores. Ernest drops the cages back over the side, hoping for more lobsters than crabs in tomorrow's catch.

from E N L L I

We get it through troughs and rainbows

falling and flying, falling and flying

rocked in an eggshell
over drowned mountain ranges.

The island swings towards us, slowly.

We slide in on an oiled keel,
step ashore with birth-wet, wind-red faces
wiping the salt from our eyes
and notice sudden, welling
quiet, and how here the breeze
lets smells of growing things
settle and breathe warmth, a host of presences
drowsing, their wings too fine to see.

There's a green track, lined with meadowsweet.
Stone houses, ramparts to the weather
Small fields that run all one way
to the sea, inviting feet
to make new paths to their own
discovered places.

After supper, lamplight
soft as the sheen of buttercups
and candle-shadow blossoms
bold on the bedroom wall.

Christine Evans

12 THE LONG ROUTE TO LUNDY

Picking up speed with the whole length of Wales to travel

WE STARTED THIS JOURNEY, this sail around the coast of Wales, many weeks ago, intending to make Lundy Island our first stop along the way. Lying just off the Devon coast it is only a day's sailing from Penarth. But when wind and foul weather conspired against us we changed plans and sailed west to Tenby instead. I don't want to miss the island, and so, with Bardsey now behind us, Lundy is to be our final destination. The trouble is, we are at the other end of Wales and Lundy lies a long way distant.

On a good day you can drive the full length of Wales, from north to south, in around four hours, provided no tractors or HGVs get in the way. Yet to sail the length of the country, from the tip of the Llŷn Peninsula in the north to the mouth of Milford Haven in the south, takes the best part of a day and a night – and that's in gentle wind conditions.

Even on a calm evening the Irish Sea is a forbidding place. The coastal lighthouses stand bright and blazing against the landmass behind, the pin pricks of yellow and white light clearly marking the dark and empty coastline of Cardigan Bay. Off Strumble Head, tankers lie silently waiting for dawn and the tide before making their way into the port of Milford Haven. The tankers make an awesome sight: close up, you realise just how big these ships really are.

John Hart helps with direction

Tankers moored near Strumble Head

South Bishop

Early in the morning we clear the Bishop and Clerks rocks. We ease past the South Bishop light, then the Smalls and, finally, we're into Milford Haven and the river Cleddau for the second time on our trip. Busy trawlers bustle past us on their way out to sea and the fishing grounds in the Atlantic. For us, Neyland marina is again a welcome sight. It means hot showers, fresh food, a much needed refuelling for *Mascotte* and a few hours on dry land. The waters of the marina are swimming with mullet. Shoals of fish tease the line all morning until, finally, after four long hours we get a bite – tea at last.

Neyland is a curious mix of workboats, fishing craft, diving platforms and expensive yachts and power boats. My brothers Huw and Richard and I used to spend hours around here as children. We would regularly row from Lawrenny upstream, back to Hobbs Point in Pembroke Dock.

With Huw at Lawrenny

Often the rowing was not done by choice but because the second-hand outboard motor on our dinghy had exploded once again.

I remember the three of us joining children from all over south Pembrokeshire after school one night in 1970, rushing to see the broken girders of the Cleddau Bridge as they lay in the river. The construction of the bridge had been nearing completion and as one of the box girders was being cantilevered into position it fell. Several men died in the accident. The bridge has been rebuilt for many years now.

Before the bridge, crossing the Cleddau meant a journey on a wonderful old car ferry. It was a trip that almost everyone in Pembroke Dock and Neyland took regularly. It was atmospheric and exciting and

Cleddau bridge   *photo Martin Cavaney*

photo Martin Cavaney   Neyland Marina in sunshine

the names of the ferry boats – the *Cleddau King*, *Cleddau Queen*, *The Alumchine* – are still imprinted on my memory.

After a night in Neyland we cast off at a quarter to nine and motor back down the Haven. At the Heads, just before the open sea, the army range patrol vessel orders us to keep 6 miles off the Castlemartin ranges. It feels like we've been here and done this before. We set *Mascotte's* sails – mainsail, jib and topsail – and, in blazing sunshine, make for Lundy Island in light winds.

At 1300 we pass St Gowan's buoy, then there is nothing but blue for hours – no boats and no land. John and Margaret Hart spend the day trying to teach me sailor's knots, with limited success.

After an idyllic day's sailing across the mouth of the Bristol Channel we finally reach Lundy. On the fishing line over the stern, four mackerel provide us with supper. It might be a scavenging fish but there is no taste quite like it, particularly after a long day in the open air.

Lundy is the most remote island we've been to, the furthest from the mainland and, perhaps, also the most beautiful. We anchor near the

A knot-tying lesson

slipway, sheltered by steep cliffs beneath the lighthouse, along with a few other boats and some distant seals for company. The bay is regularly washed by white sweeps of light from Lundy's north lighthouse and, in the distance, weaker flashes from Bull Point on the English mainland.

Next morning we take the tender to the shore. By now I've been on *Mascotte* for several weeks and such isolation can induce all sorts of hallucinations. My sighting of a beautiful mermaid sitting on a rock turns out to be Susie Ballerstedt, the assistant keeper on Lundy, waiting for the passenger boat and another day's deluge of visitors. This is Susie's job for the summer. In my mind, after just three minutes of talking to her, I have mapped out the rest of her life – with

Approaching Lundy at last

me. But to no avail. She has passengers to look after, and I have an island to explore.

A swarm of quad bikes, Land Rovers and tractors arrive on the jetty at the same time as the Ilfracombe boat noses into the bay. Dozens of eager day-trippers clutch their binoculars, cameras and anoraks and hurry off up the hill. The crew members watch them go and then start to load Lundy's post and other exports.

It's a steep pull up to the top of the island and most visitors head straight for the 'Marisco Tavern' to recover from the climb. The pub has an old sign advertising pickled gulls' eggs for 2d. The landlady, Jenny Clarke, left a grown-up family on the mainland for life on Lundy. Her daughter Joanne has followed Jenny here for the summer.

'I work as a chambermaid, looking after the rooms,' she says. 'You'd be surprised at the number of people who

Lundy was once inhabited by Vikings, probably as a winter base for marauding armies, but it lay in the hands of the Marisco family for many years. The remains of the Marisco Castle can still be seen on the island – it was the stronghold of this powerful and ruthless family. The Marisco ownership ended when Henry III hanged William de Marisco for piracy.

With *Mascotte* at anchor, Jon Rees is rowed out in the tender for some night-time filming

Susie Ballerstedt, assistant keeper

Jenny Clarke

Joanne Clarke

come out here for a holiday. And do you know something? My social life is far better out here than it ever was on the mainland.'

You really do get a sense of community on Lundy. In a corner of the tavern the crew of a visiting yacht devours lunch. It's as if they haven't eaten for days. They go back for another helping. Perhaps they're laying in supplies for the next leg of their journey.

Lundy rises sharply to a height of 400 feet and is dominated by a huge deserted lighthouse. It was built too high, so that when a mist came down its warning light was above the blanketing fog and not visible from the sea. That first lighthouse has now been replaced by three smaller ones on the edges of the island. Climbing to the top of the old lighthouse is no mean feat for someone in my condition. In the old lamp-room two decrepit wooden chairs tempt a breathless man and I'm glad to sit down and recover.

Today the view from here is spectacular. Below the lighthouse lies an ancient graveyard. It's only from this height that you can see the flat gravestones outside the cemetery walls, slabs that mark the last resting places of mariners of uncertain religion. They are clearly outsiders to the last in this smallest of communities. Out in the distance, beyond the

Old Lighthouse, Lundy

Shutter Rock on Lundy has seen the fatal demise of many fine ships, ranging from a Spanish galleon that sailed with the Armada to the massive pre-dreadnought battleship *Montagu*. The rock features in Kingsley's *Westward Ho* as the scene of the wreck of the *Santa Catharina*. Whilst there is no record of deliberate wrecking on the coast of Lundy, the inhabitants of the island were certainly happy to make use of 'the harvest of the sea', plundering wrecks.

cluster of cottages, walkers – miniature and shapeless – criss-cross the island in timetabled relaxation, eager to get their money's worth before the Ilfracombe boat departs.

The battleship *Montagu* went ashore here in a dense fog in 1906, driving onto the rocks of Shutter Point on the south-west corner of the island. The captain and navigation officer thought they had hit Hartland Point on the Devon coast. Two officers scaled the cliff to find help and presented themselves to the keeper of the northern lighthouse. They tried to tell him that they were on the mainland. A brief but furious debate took place, with the keeper finishing the discussion with the simple but succinct comment that he knew 'which bloody light was his'.

All efforts to free the *Montagu* from the rocks failed dismally and, eventually, she had to be broken up where she lay. The shattered remains of her hull were battered to pieces by the wind

Making for the Old Lighthouse, with cameraman Jon Rees and director Sara Allen

and ever-present sea. As late as 1945 you could still see bits of the giant warship at the bottom of the cliff but now all traces of her have gone.

At the far end of Lundy, in a stone cottage borrowed from a fairy tale, lives Anne Westcott. She's been coming to Lundy for several decades and shows me her divining rods which, she claims, can pick out ancient burial grounds.

'For lots of people, Lundy marks the convergence of ley lines from all the spiritual sites,' she says. 'Right across the country.'

I assume she's slightly batty until she makes me take the rods. They leap into life. There's a magic about this island that I don't understand. Anne smiles knowingly at her convert.

The 'Marisco Tavern' comes alive at night. The yacht crew from lunchtime are here again, in fine spirits. Now they're on to dinner and they'll probably be here for breakfast. This is a pub where fathers and sons, mothers and daughters, all sit under the same roof. Two musicians play accordian and flute for the crowd and keep going during the power cut. There are no last orders and no worry about getting home.

This is my last night of island life and like so many times before on this journey I feel as if I've walked back into the 1950s. There are few cars, everyone says hello to you, whether you know them or not, and people leave their belongings around the place without worrying about

During the reign of King James I, Lundy was renowned for its pirates. They were well organised and led by a man called Salkeld – for years no ship could sail up or down the Bristol Channel without fear of being captured or sunk by the Lundy pirates. Despite Royal Commissions and petitions, the pirates continued with their riotous careers until the reign of Queen Anne.

The graveyard enclosure – and grave slabs outside its walls

theft. There is an unreality about the islands and the people who live on them – but there's nothing wrong with that. On the contrary, I quite like fantasy islands.

At some dark hour we row across the bay to *Mascotte* and slip easily into our bunks. In the morning, with the anchor chain hauled up, we set a course for Swansea and home. It is the end of my summer journey around the coast of Wales. I've visited six islands and travelled four hundred miles. I've encountered some of the most fascinating people you could ever hope to meet.

Visiting the islands of Wales has been something of a return to childhood. As kids we were kept occupied during so many summer holidays by day trips to the islands off the Welsh coast. There always seemed to be a long-awaited boat journey in halcyon weather – baking sunshine and warm breezes, voyages that we never wanted to end. The journeys were always followed by a scramble over rocks that were inviting and spectacular. Then it was home in time for tea.

Years later, those islands are still places of magic for me. They may no longer be sites of pilgrimage, like they once were in ancient times, but ask any visitor to Lundy or Bardsey, Caldey or Ramsey, what they are searching for and they will tell you. They're in search of a place beyond the sea, a place that's good for the soul. And in the islands around the coast of Wales they – and I – have found what we're all looking for.

Lundy's beautiful clifftops

SHIPPING FORECAST: WESTERLY 4 OR 5,
DECREASING 3 FOR A TIME.
MAINLY GOOD.

13 SAILING HOME

I'M GLAD TO BE ABLE TO SAY I've sailed round Wales twice – John Hart, our pilot aboard *Mascotte* smiles when I mention this fact.

'You can understand a country better from the sea,' he says.

Before the age of the railway and the car, visitors to this country would be much more familiar with our coast, our harbours and ports, than we are today. Sailing around Wales, you get a different perspective of its size, its shape, colour and smell.

Halfway between Lundy and Swansea, Sara Allen, the director of our television series, shouts that phrase so beloved of television types.

'It's a wrap,' she calls.

It's the end of our shoot to make *Magic Islands*. We've spent weeks together over the summer, filming and sailing. A week ago I'd have cheered at Sara's words. For days on end I'd been damp from spray. And of course it had rained a little too much, even for Wales in the summer. For a while I had started to regret offering to film the islands of Wales as a complete journey: why had I not gone for the option of being shipped in for a few walking shots, then heading safely home?

This afternoon, however, it seems as if the weather is teasing us – showing us how baking hot and beautiful the Welsh coast can be on a good day. At the moment none of us wants this journey to end. It is

There are over one hundred islands and islets around the coast of Wales. This includes well-known places like Anglesey, Bardsey and Skomer; it also includes little-known islands like Ynys Gorad Goch, St Tudwals and Sully Island.

truly idyllic, lying on a scorched wooden deck gazing up into cream sails set against a blue sky – a good time for a kip and to reflect on running away to sea.

What this journey has most impressed on me is the wonderful sensation of time. When you live your life, as most of us do, governed by exact times to get up and go to work – squeezing in a window of ten minutes for this or for that – to go home, to go to bed, you begin to realise the extraordinary strain by which most of us

Homeward bound

live our lives. Sailing changes all that. The tides and weather take control, and there's nothing you can do to change that. Each day, nature decides your progress – or lack of it.

The islanders we met on our cruise were a fascinating bunch of people – but who would want to go and live on an island off Wales? I can understand running away to the Caribbean or a Greek Island. But why Wales? The answer is, I guess, our islands offer a familiarity, a diluted wilderness, an Eden not too far from home. The islands offer an escape from the rat race of the mainland but an escape within easy reach of helicopters should things go wrong. Many islanders admitted to me that they were running away from something – from rogue bosses, bad marriages or relationships, or some hurtful experience associated with the mainland. The islands offer a strange kind of balm.

Living on an island is harsh and unforgiving for the most part. And for those escaping other people, island life sharply accentuates interdependence. But for all that, I've yet to spend time in the company of so many well-adjusted, well-sorted men and women. It's as though living on an island

Will, hauling in the sails

brings you to terms with who you are, like no other experience does. If people are influenced by their surroundings, then these rocky outcrops must be amongst the most beautiful places to live anywhere on earth. It's difficult to stand on Ramsey, for example, and look out over fields and sea and not feel that all is well with the world.

Sailing round the islands and coast of Wales is like flicking through the chapters of our history. Each generation's scars are left on the ground. From prehistoric standing stones to the cold chimneys left by yesterday's industrialists, remains of the past all pass before you. I wonder if future travellers will gaze upon our nuclear installations or oil refineries with a similar sense of lost heritage?

Many of the Welsh islands can be approached on foot at low water – although you need to take care not to be cut off by the advancing tide. Places that can be reached like this include Sully Island, close to Cardiff, Gateholm in Pembrokeshire and Burry Holmes on Gower.

From the water you can see how beautiful yet fragile our coast really is. Coastal communities in Wales desperately need tourism, yet by covering the cliffs in caravans you destroy the very thing visitors come to see in the first place. Powerboats speed in for a closer look at the seals and puffins on the Pembrokeshire islands and with screaming engines scare the animals and birds that make the area so precious.

On our cruise we dropped into places like Little Haven and Abersoch on weekends to see little seaside villages gridlocked by snarling traffic.

Will on the bowsprit

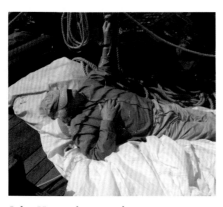

John Hart, relaxing at last

Preserving these communities in aspic is no solution and I don't pretend to have the answers but a better balance seems to be required. Sailing homewards now, though, I am content to leave the political arguments over planning and inward migration to others. Mine has been a rare experience, the chance to watch the islands and the coast of Wales close up during the course of one brief summer. And after it all, you can only conclude that something precious is endangered and needs to be carefully cherished.

Mascotte's owner Tony Winter has never sailed round Wales before, and is quietly pleased that the old girl hasn't put a foot wrong. Will, his son, is getting married in a few weeks, and has had his fill of jokes about his last days of freedom. John and Maggs Hart, our pilot and navigator, have sailed around the world but agree there has been a certain magic about the places and people we have met on this trip. This hasn't been a journey of epic proportions across oceans or continents, but a voyage around the people and places we call home. Six islands and four hundred miles.

On a summer's evening, lying in the sun, looking up at the mainsail, we're heading home.

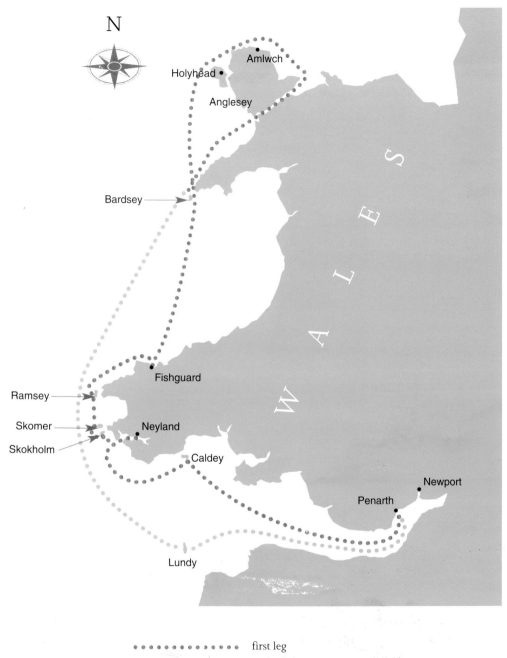

N

Amlwch
Holyhead
Anglesey

Bardsey

Fishguard

Ramsey
Skomer
Neyland
Skokholm
Caldey

Newport
Penarth

Lundy

• • • • • • • • • • first leg
• • • • • • • • • • return leg

A MAP OF OUR VOYAGE